THE AVENGERS AND NEW AVENGERS COLLECTIBLES

John Buss

AMBERLEY

Acknowledgements

I would like to thank the following for their assistance in the preparation of this book: Louise Harker at Vectis Toy Auctions, the David Oliver / www.moviebilia.co.uk collection, and Warner Todd Huston.

First published 2019

Amberley Publishing
The Hill, Stroud
Gloucestershire, GL5 4EP

www.amberley-books.com

Copyright © John Buss, 2019

The right of John Buss to be identified as the Author of this work has been asserted in accordance with the Copyrights, Designs and Patents Act 1988.

ISBN 978 1 4456 8886 2 (print)
ISBN 978 1 4456 8887 9 (ebook)

British Library Cataloguing in Publication Data.
A catalogue record for this book is available from the British Library.

Typeset in 10pt on 13pt Celeste.
Origination by Amberley Publishing.
Printed in the UK.

Contents

Introduction   4

Books and Annuals   5

Toys   22

Magazines and Comics   28

Records   40

Fashion, etc.   50

Promotional and other items   55

The New Avengers   61

Books / Annuals   62

Toys and Games   72

Magazines / Comics   85

Miscellaneous items   88

Records   92

Introduction

What can be said about what is probably 'the' fantasy adventure series of the 1960s?

The series debuted on 7 January 1961 and was broadcast live, no possibility of re-takes – whatever happened, right or wrong, it went out on air. The series was much drier in the beginning, with little of the wit that was to become one of its trademarks. In those early days, it featured a much more serious Cops and Robbers format, revolving around the main character of Dr David Keel (Ian Hendry).

The premise was set up in the first episode, 'Hot Snow'. After the murder of Dr Keel's fiancé by drug dealers and the police's inability to act due to lack of evidence, Dr Keel vows to 'Avenge' her death by tracking down her killers. Hence the title *The Avengers*. In the course of so doing, Keel is approached and questioned by Steed (Patrick Macnee), a mysterious undercover agent, who then assists in the task. Thus the original team was formed.

After Ian Hendry left at the end of the first season he was followed by a stream of lovely but dangerous ladies including Cathy Gale (Honor Blackman), Emma Peel (Diana Rigg) and Tara King (Linda Thorson), who took Keel's place as Steed's sidekicks. Increasingly outrageous storylines and fantasy elements developed during the 161 episodes, made during its six seasons.

Although the series had nearly a nine year run, effectively spanning a whole decade (1961–69), most items of *Avengers* merchandise were issued in a two-year period, 1966–67. This coincided with (for many) the show's most popular pairing, that of John Steed and Emma Peel. This is a series that continues to influence even today. Cathy Gale and Emma Peel were the first in a long line of emancipated heroines with influences still being seen in many modern series.

Books and Annuals

The first book, solely based upon *The Avengers,* was this novel featuring the pairing of Steed and Cathy Gale. (This is the only original novel to feature Cathy Gale.) It was published by Consul Books, a division of World Distributors, a company probably better known for the vast array of TV-related annuals it produced throughout the sixties, seventies and eighties. As with all the paperbacks issued in connection with *The Avengers,* this is a totally new adventure using only the characters from the show. This was originally sold at a price of 2s 6d.

The Avengers by Douglas Enefer, Consul Books, 1963.

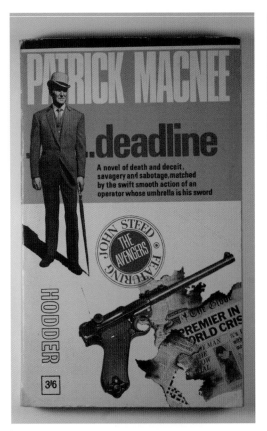

Above left: *Dead Line* paperback.

Above right: *Dead Duck* paperback.

Left: *The Floating Game,* UK issue.

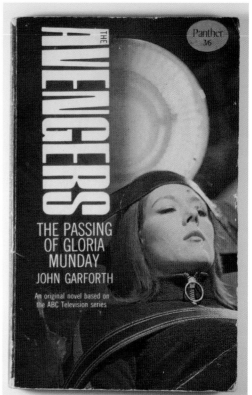

Above left: The Laugh was on Lazarus, UK issue.

Above right: The Passing of Gloria Munday, UK issue.

Right: Heil Harris!, UK issue.

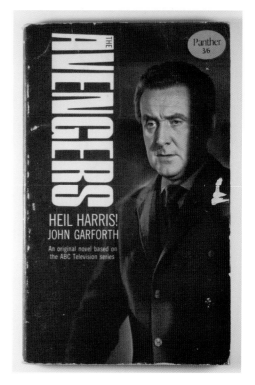

The next two books to appear were from Hodder & Stoughton, and were written by the show's star Patrick Macnee, with, according to a small acknowledgement inside each book, the assistance of Peter Leslie. Though primarily billed as John Steed adventures, both books feature Emma Peel. These two books were entitled *Deadline* and *Dead Duck* respectively and both titles were published in 1965 with a cover price of 3s 6d. These books were also re-issued in the late 1990s by Titan Books.

Two years later in 1967, yet another publisher entered the fray, when Panther Books produced four titles based on the series. All four titles were written by John Garforth and featured the pairing of John Steed and Emma Peel. They were issued at a cover price of 3s 6d. The four books were entitled *The Floating Game, The Laugh was on Lazarus, The Passing of Gloria Munday* and *Heil Harris!*

American Paperbacks

Starting with reissues of the four UK Panther books in 1967, in the US Berkley Medallion Books published a total of nine books based on the series. All hit the shelves at a cover price of 60 cents each. There were two different editions of these first four John Garforth books in America. The first US editions of numbers one through four featured a single large photograph from the series, while the second edition had two smaller photographs on the cover.

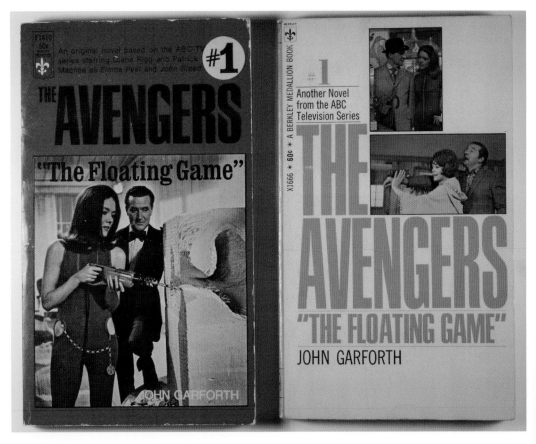

The Floating Game, US issues.

The Laugh was on Lazarus,
US issues.

The Passing of Gloria Munday,
US issues.

Heil Harris!, US issues.

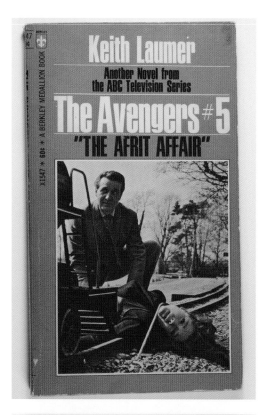

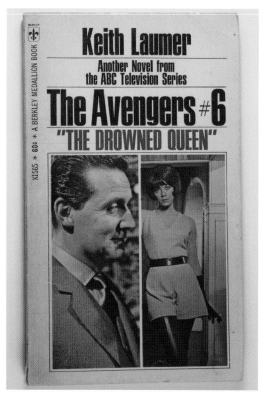

Above left: The Afrit Affair.

Above right: The Drowned Queen.

Left: The Gold Bomb.

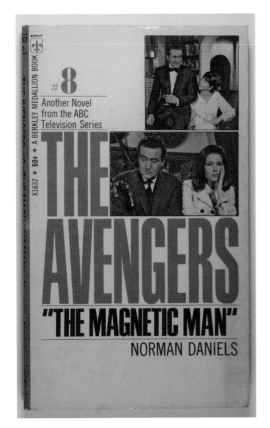

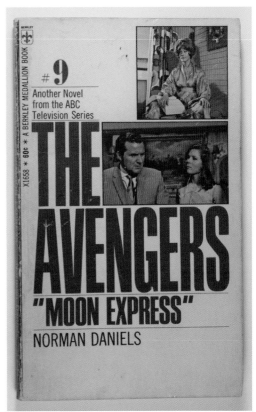

Above left: The Magnetic Man.

Above right: The Moon Express.

Having published these John Garforth books, Berkley Medallion then proceeded to continue the series with a further five titles, none of which saw publication in the UK. The first book, *The Afrit Affair*, also featured Emma Peel, but the subsequent four featured the new pairing of Steed and Tara King. Although, for some strange reason, the covers of *Moon Express* and *Magnetic Man* show photographs of Steed and Emma, she does not feature in either book. The same can be said of the second American edition of *The Passing of Gloria Munday*, an Emma Peel adventure yet Tara is on the cover!

Books five to seven in the American series, *The Afrit Affair, The Drowned Queen,* and *The Gold Bomb*, were all written by Keith Laumer and published in 1968.

Finally, the eighth and ninth books in the series, *The Magnetic Man* and *The Moon Express*, were written by Norman Daniels and were published in 1969.

Portuguese Paperbacks

The original two Patrick Macnee / Peter Leslie books were translated into Portuguese by M. M. Ferreira da Silva and published in Portugal by Deaga, *Deadline* becoming *Os Vingadores: O Dia Depois De Amanha*, while *Dead Duck* translated as *Os Vingadores: O Pato Morto*. Unfortunately, copies of neither book could be located in time to include images.

Solar Books in France published the four John Garforth books under the following titles in 1967, all four being translated into French by Marie Watkins: *Le Flambeur Flambé – The Floating Game*; *Drôles de Morts – The Laugh was on Lazarus*; *Pop-Crime – The Passing of Gloria Munday*; *Heil Harris! – Heil Harris!*

The Floating Game, French issue.

The Laugh was on Lazarus, French issue.

Above left: *The Passing of Gloria Munday*, French issue.

Above right: *Heil Harris!*, French issue.

Dutch Paperbacks

The four John Garforth books were all published by Zwarte beertjes in the Netherlands under the following titles: *Maling aan de Maffia – The Floating Game* (published in 1968); *Lijken in Actie – The Laugh was on Lazarus* (published in 1968); *Het heengaan van Gloria Munday – The Passing of Gloria Munday* (published in 1970); *Heil Harris – Heil Harris!* (published in 1970).

A fifth Dutch paperback was produced, though strictly speaking it is more akin to the British annuals by Atlas which are detailed later in this book, being roughly the same size. It was produced by Vanderhout & Co. N. V. in 1968 and is a strange mishmash of the British annuals from 1967 and 1968. At a quick glance you could be forgiven in thinking it was just a translated version of the 1968 Tara King annual. Take a closer look at the cover and you'll notice that the illustrations on the cover, which on the original UK annual showed Tara King, have been subtly altered to make them look more like Emma Peel. This book's contents also do not match the cover, having instead come from the 1967 Emma Peel annual along with an abbreviated version of the feature 'Clothes make the Man' from the 1968 annual. Another difference is that unlike the UK annuals, the stories are featured in full colour.

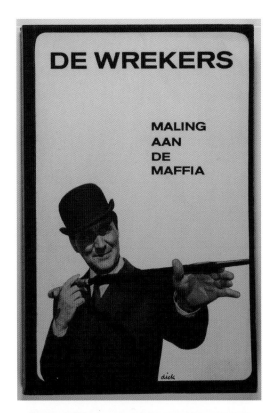

Above left: *The Floating Game,* Dutch issue.

Above right: *The Laugh was on Lazarus,*
Dutch issue.

Left: *The Passing of Gloria Munday,*
Dutch issue.

Above left: *Heil Harris!* Dutch issue.

Above right: Dutch *Annual*.

German Books

Only three of the John Garforth titles saw publication in Germany and the German titles are considerably different to their UK versions when translated back into English. The German editions, published by Hayne in 1967, were *The Floating Game* which became *Drie Kleine Chinamadchen*, which literally means 'Three Little Chinese Girls'. This was translated by

The Floating Game, German issue.

Above left: The Laugh was on Lazarus,
German issue.

Above right: The Passing of Gloria
Munday, German issue.

Left: German omnibus.

Elisabeth Simon. The second German paperback, *The Laugh was on Lazarus*, translated by Fritz Moeglich, became *Die Traurigen Toten von Highgate* or in English 'The Sad Corpses of Highgate'. The final German paperback, *Der Singende tod Von Blackpool*, 'The Singing Death of Blackpool', translated by Wolf Heckmann, had started out as *The Passing of Gloria Munday*. These Three German paperbacks also saw publication as a hardback omnibus edition released by Hayne in 1967.

Chilean Paperbacks

Interestingly, the four John Garforth books also saw release in Chile in 1968, having been translated by Lina Larran, the publishers being Zig Zag. They were issued under the following titles: *Juegos Flotantes – The Floating Game; Se Rieron de Lazaro – The Laugh was on Lazarus; La Muerto de Gloria Munday – The Passing of Gloria Munday; Peligro Mortal – Heil Harris!*

Above left: *The Floating Game*, Chilean issue.

Above right: *The Laugh was on Lazarus*, Chilean issue.

Heil Harris!, Chilean issue.

British Annuals

Three annuals were produced in the UK for *The Avengers* by Atlas Publishing. The first of the annuals published in 1967 (though no year is given on the cover of any of these annuals), is the only one to feature Mrs Peel. At a publication price of 10*s* 6*d,* this is probably the nicest of the three annuals to have been produced by Atlas. It contains a good mixture of text and strip stories, these having been written by Peter Leslie and illustrated by John Stokes. Also contained, however, are some very nice features that include behind-the-scenes photos from some of the classic Emma Peel stories. The annual's front cover shows Steed and Emma fighting with two assailants on a stone stairway, while the back cover is just plain yellow.

The next *Avengers* annual to be produced was in 1968, once again no year on the cover, and was the first of two annuals to feature Tara King. The cover for this one is red, with a head and shoulders drawing of Steed and two smaller drawings of Tara and Steed below this. Both the front and back covers are the same. As with the previous annual it contained a mixture of stories and features. The publication price remained the same as the previous year annual at 10*s* 6*d.*

The last of the original *Avengers* annuals was produced the following year in 1969, and once again there is no indication of the year to be found on the cover. As with the previous year, this annual features Tara King. With the publication price remaining the same at

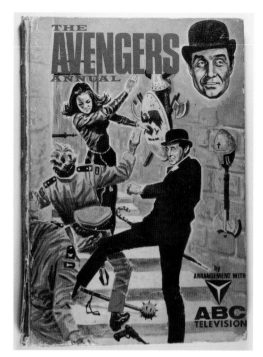

Above left: UK *Annual 1*.

Above right: UK *Annual 2*.

Right: UK *Annual 3*.

10s 6d, a similar mixture of stories and features to the previous year's made up the annual's contents. The cover shows a full face drawing of Steed with Tara looking over his left shoulder, with smaller action-type images and what looks like an explosion forming the background. Both front and back covers show this same image.

Many other British annuals also contained features, stories or references to the series. Following are details of just a few:

The first notable book was *TV Crimebusters* published by TV Publications Ltd in 1962. This is notable as among its contents, it included an *Avengers* strip 'The Drug Pedlar'. This is the only known publication to contain an Ian Hendry *Avengers* story. It is also interesting in the combined use of photographs and illustrations in the production of this strip story. This annual-sized book, priced at 8s 6d, also used the same technique for similar strip stories of other shows such as *Danger Man*.

Two Odhams Press-published *Star TV & Film Annuals* included contents relevant to the series. The 1966 annual contained a short feature with photographs about Honor Blackman. While the 1967 annual included a feature about the ABC TV casting director Dodo Watts, which referenced the series with photograph of Diana Rigg as Mrs Peel. Both annuals had a publication price of 12s.

The publishers Purnell put out both a *Television Show Book* and a *Television Star Book* in 1964. The first, published at a price of 10s 6d, included photographs and a feature on *The Avengers*, while the second, which featured an article and photographs of the show's star Patrick Macnee, cost less than half of the first at only 5s. Purnell also featured *The Avengers* in its 1965 *Television Show Book* and 1967 *Television Stars Book*.

The children's paper *TV Comic* featured the *Avengers* at several times over the years (more details later), with the series also featuring in several of the comics' annuals. The first

 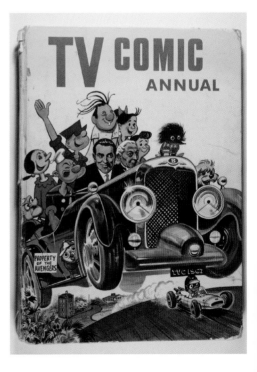

Above left: TV Crimebusters Annual.

Above right: TV Comic Annual, 1967.

of these was the *TV Comic Annual* 1967. This annual also featured Steed on the cover, at the wheel of his Bentley – with the first Doctor, William Hartnell, among his passengers. Inside the annual are two, four-page-long, untitled black and white strip stories featuring Emma Peel. This sold at a price of 9*s* 6*d*.

The Avengers didn't feature in the *TV Comic Annual* again until the 1970 annual, which included an *Avengers* text story with Steed and Tara King, entitled 'In Fable Land'. The original price for this annual 10*s* 6*d*.

The series also featured in the following year's *TV Comic Annual* (1971) with, once again, a Steed and Tara King *Avengers* text story, 'The Spirits of Christmas'. Publication price for the annual this year had increased though, to 12*s*.

The Avengers would be absent from the 1972 *TV Comic Annual,* but returned in the 1973 annual with another strip story featuring Steed and Tara King, entitled 'The Woodland Folk'. The original price for this annual was 65p in new money.

Honor Blackman's Book of Self Defence by Honor Blackman with Joe and Doug Robinson. Now, while not directly related to the series, this publication is worth mentioning as it is unlikely it would have appeared if Honor Blackman had not been such a success in both the *Avengers* and the James Bond movie, *Goldfinger*. The book is packed with photographs of Honor demonstrating various self-defence techniques. There appear to be at least three different editions of this book. The first UK edition was published in hardback by Andre Deutsch Ltd in 1965, while the second UK edition was published as a paperback by Penguin Books in 1967. There was also an American edition, though details for this are unknown at present.

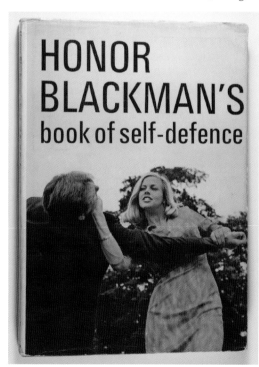 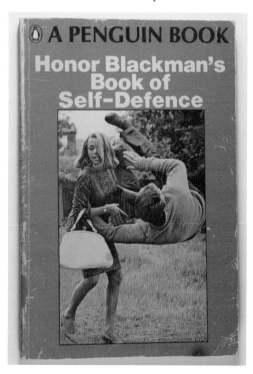

Above left: *Book of Self Defence* hardback.

Above right: *Book of Self Defence* paperback.

Toys

Avengers Gift Set (GS 40), Corgi Toys, 1966

Produced between 1966 and 1969, this is probably one of the most desirable pieces of *Avengers* memorabilia. Originally issued at a price of 16s 9d in 1966, with the price rising to 16s 11d the following year, the set contained two die-cast models. One was a red 1927 Bentley and the second was a white Lotus Elan S2, which had an opening bonnet, tipping seats and sliding windows.

The Bentley used in this set was just a further re-use of a model that was already in Corgi's Classics range, while the Lotus was also an existing model in the standard range. To further complement the set, it came with a seated figure of Steed in a grey suit, with a standing figure of Mrs Peel dressed in a white trouser suit. Also included were three small black plastic umbrellas.

Over the years there has been much debate over the colour of Steed's Bentley in the set. Officially, the model was only ever issued in red with black mudguards and silver or gold spoked wheels, but it is not that clear cut. Early issues of the set did see release containing a green Bentley with red spoked wheels and green mudguards. Now, this model is a little bit of a hybrid of the two original Corgi Classics issues of the Bentley, as there were both green and red issues of that model in the range. The green issue, however, had silver or gold wheels, while the red issue had red wheels. In short, any green version of the Bentley in the gift set should have both green mudguards and red wheels. Any other green version of the Bentley appearing in a set, has probably been substituted from either a Corgi Classics issue or the

Corgi Gift Set, green (Vectis).

Corgi Gift Set, red.

World of Wooster set issued in 1967. The World of Wooster issue Bentley can be distinguished by its gunmetal-coloured mudguards and dark red interior; all issues of the *Avengers* Bentley have a brown interior. One other notable thing about the World of Wooster issue is that this also features an identical driving figure to *The Avengers* set; identical, that is, except for colour. While the Steed figure was in a grey suit the Jeeves figure is in a black suit.

In a 1998 interview, Corgi's chief designer Marcel Van Cleemput was asked about the Avengers gift set and the colour variations. He had this to say: 'Well, yes we already had the Bentley, I think we had the Lotus as well. But that was a very popular series on television. In the series, it was green and our model was red because we'd already got a green Bentley in our Classics range and I think, just to put it green in with that would have reduced our sales considerably because kids would have said, well I've got the green Bentley. You have to; it's like an artist's license like painters do. We were in Northampton where all the design and development tooling were done, production was in Swansea and sometimes Swansea production, if they were short of a colour paint, would to expedite things would do a few things we didn't know about until it was too late. We issued a specification sheet for each job, denoting colour and everything and it should have been abided by.'

With the advent of so-called 'restoration' of Corgi models, or repaints, and the increased quality of reproduction boxes, it has become an increasing problem trying to discern originals from those trying to deceive, a task that is now virtually impossible with the plastic umbrellas from this set. While early reproductions were produced either in white metal or resin, both of which were fairly easy to distinguish from an original, these are now being reproduced in injection moulded plastic exactly the same as the originals.

John Steed Bowler Hat, Lone Star (Die-Cast Machine Tools Ltd), 1966

This, apparently, was a child's felt bowler hat, 'A replica of the very smart "City" bowler hat worn by John Steed.' Supposedly, it came supplied with a 'Steed' label. This must surely have been a must have for any young *Avengers* fan. While this appeared in the 1966 Lone Star catalogue, the author has never come across a verified example of this product, in nearly forty years of collecting.

Sword stick.

John Steed Sword Stick, Lone Star (Die-Cast Machine Tools Ltd), 1966

A plastic swordstick, which could also be used as a water pistol! To quote the Lone Star catalogue for 1966, 'This has tremendous play value. All plastic – a "Cane handle walking stick" that is really a sword in a scabbard. The ferrule or tip has a slight recess (for corks) with a pinhole (for water). The sword is fitted with a safety tip, which acts as a washer which is the secret behind the cork firing and water squirting features in the stick!!' Well that should explain it all. This was Lone Star's answer to Steed's famous sword stick umbrella from the series and was presented on a colourful backing card depicting Steed brandishing a sword stick.

Emma Peel Doll, Fairylite, 1966–7

In around 1966, a 10-inch high plastic doll of Mrs Peel was released. While there is no manufacture's name on the box, the box is just copy-written 'ABC Television 1966', having been made in Hong Kong. It is believed to have been produced by Fairylite. It came dressed in black plastic trousers, a short black woollen coat, black roll-neck sweater and black plastic boots. Also contained was a plastic base and a metal strut to support the doll when standing, along with two further outfits for the doll. These were a pair of brown plastic trousers, a black wool pair of trousers, a white plastic tunic, a black plastic coat, a white plastic rain hat with black trim, also a pair of black mittens. Coming in a yellow box, with black lettering proclaiming '*The Avengers* Emma Peel Doll', the box had a clear plastic window through which the doll could be seen, holding a gun in its right hand. This is also a good indication of the doll being a genuine Mrs Peel doll, as there is a small lug in the palm of the doll's hand which enables the doll to hold onto the gun. This issue of the doll has also been seen with a white jumper and grey wool trousers. Original price was 19s 11d. In around the mid-1980s, what appeared to be a second issue of this doll appeared in collecting circles, now widely believed to be an unlicensed fake. The box proclaimed The New Emma Peel Doll and was issued in a different costume to those mentioned above.

Emma Peel doll.

Tara King Doll, unknown manufacture, Japan

This is another example of a likely unlicensed and non-contemporary action doll. Examples of this doll first seem to have appeared around the mid-to-late 1990s. The doll is a very crude, cheap-looking plastic figure of similar size to the Emma Peel figure. It has a roundish face with a bob of black hair. This appears to have come in a plain brown card box, with flaps at either end, with the words 'Tara King Doll' stamped on the box front. Around the same time, previously unknown similar dolls appeared for characters from other sixties TV and film shows, including Agent 99 from *Get Smart* and Yeoman Janice Rand from *Star Trek*. It is quite probable that while the dolls used are indeed original 1960s dolls, they were not issued as these characters at the time and some enterprising individual has repackaged them as such in more recent times.

Likewise, Emma Peel and Cathy Gale guns that are neither of 1960s issue nor licensed products have appeared in recent years.

The Avengers Jigsaws, Thomas, Hope & Sankey, 1966

A set of four jigsaw puzzles were produced for sale in Woolworths in the UK by the firm Thomas, Hope & Sankey in 1966 at an original price of 2s 9d each. The puzzles were 11 inch x 17 inch in size and each contained approximately 340 pieces. All four puzzles featured the Steed / Mrs Peel pairing fighting various assailants and were based very loosely on episodes from the series. The four puzzles are 'No Escape', 'Castle De'ath', 'In the Basement', and 'Archery Practice'.

Avengers jigsaw 1.

Avengers jigsaw box back.

Avengers jigsaw 3.

Avengers jigsaw 4.

Shooting Game, Merit toys, 1967

The firm of J. & L. Randall Ltd, also known as Merit, produced a shooting game in 1967. This was basically a very nicely illustrated card backdrop with a spring loaded action, which came with a plastic gun which fired suction tip darts. The intention was that you fired said darts at the centrally placed illustration of a crate of dynamite, which, when hit, would cause the villain's car to 'explode' – well, spring off the target's base. This was not the only shooting game to be produced by Merit. They also created a near identical game for the Roger Moore *Saint* series, which instead of a car featured a boat. For what this toy consists of, its original asking price of 18s 6d seems quite pricey.

A few other items were licensed by the show's producers but appear not to have been produced. These included 'A Shooting round Corners Gun', for which Chad Valley took out a license in 1965. Also licensed by other companies but not produced were 'View them yourself' slides, an *Avengers* Bagatelle set and an 'Emma Peel Dress Cut-out Book'.

Merit Shooting Game.

Magazines and Comics

Asides from the obvious *TV Times* covers and features (some of these will be detailed later) *The Avengers* appeared in a whole range of different publications. Starting with comics or rather comic strips, asides from the aforementioned *TV Times*, one of the earliest appearances in print of *The Avengers* was a newspaper strip featuring Steed and Mrs Gale. This strip appears to have been published in both *Look Westward*, which appears to be a West Country equivalent of the *TV Times* as well as the Scottish equivalent, *The Viewer*, between September 1963 and May 1964. There were at least four stories published between these dates: 'Epidemic of Terror', 'Quest for a Queen', 'Operation Harem' and 'The Runaway Brain'. It appears that the same strip stories also appeared in both the *Manchester Evening News* and the *TV Post* in Northern Ireland at around the same time. These strips were to be the only appearance of the Steed and Cathy Gale pairing in this form. By far the bulk of published comic strips or even stories generally for that matter of *The Avengers* feature the John Steed and Emma Peel pairing.

The Avengers Thorp & Porter 1966

In 1966, the British publishers Thorp & Porter produced a one-issue, 68-page, black & white comic for the princely sum of 1*s* 6*d*. This comic contained four stories, all featuring Emma Peel. These four stories were 'The Mochocks', 'The K stands for Killers', 'No Jury – No Justice' and 'Deadly Efficient'. This one issue British comic would also see publication in both Holland and Germany, but not as a single publication. In the Netherlands it was published as: *TV Classics No. 2103 De Wrekers: Mohocks / De K – Club* ('The Mochocks / The K stands for Killers'); and : *TV Classics No. 2106 De Wrekers: 'n dolle rechter / Ophoog niveau!* ('No Jury – No Justice / Deadly Efficient'). While the first issue featured the same cover as the UK original, the second issue featured a new illustration featuring Steed and Mrs Peel fighting it out in court room. These reprints were published by Classics Nederland N. V. in 1967.

A third comic did appear in the Netherlands in 1970, featuring Steed and Tara King; this was *Televisie Favorieten No. 8 De Wrekers*. This series of *Televisie Favorieten* comics featured a different popular TV series in each issue. The strips in this comic appear to have been taken from the UK publication *TV Comic*, albeit slightly redrawn in several places. It is worth mentioning at this point that at least one issue of the Dutch equivalent to *TV Century 21* comic, *TV2000*, did feature a photograph of Diana Rigg as Mrs Peel (*TV2000 No. 34,* pub. 1969).

As was the case in Holland, the Thorp & Porter comic was split into two issues for its German publication, which also used the same cover art for their release. *Krimi Klassiker Nummer 1 Mit Charme, Schirm und Melone, Krimi Klassiker Nummer 2 Mit Charme, Schirm und Melone: Jagd ohne Gnade / Todliche Wirkung.*

In Germany there was, and still is, a very long-running teen magazine called *Bravo*. Throughout the sixties and seventies, this magazine continued to feature many different

Above left: UK *Avengers* comic.

Above right: Dutch comic 1.

Right: Dutch comic 2.

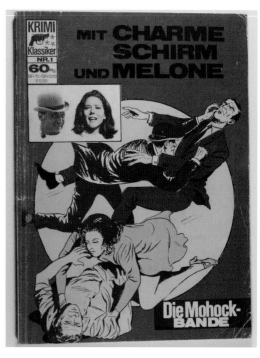

Above left: Dutch comic 3.

Above right: German comic 1.

Left: German comic 2.

TV series, *The Avengers* being no exception. Most notable about this magazine, though, is its series of *Starschnitt* or 'Star cuts'. This was a series of near-life-size, full-length portrait photographs of various stars, which would be published over several issues. Diana Rigg as Emma Peel would feature as one of these *Starschnitt* in 1967, as well as both herself and

Bravo Starschnitt.

Patrick Macnee appearing on the cover of several issues, while in 1970 the magazine also reprinted several comic strips from the British TV comic.

Meet the Avengers (Star Special 15), World Distributors, 1963

This magazine is one of a series of different magazines, each one of which focuses upon a different TV or film show or actor. Other magazines in the series featured *Z Cars*, Richard Chamberlin as *Dr Kildare*, etc. Published by World Distributors at a price of 2s 6d, this magazine is a very good introduction to the Steed and Cathy Gale series. It contains character profiles of not only Steed and Cathy, but also those of the actors who played them, along with behind the scenes looks at *Avengers* fashion and the production of an episode.

Meet the Avengers.

In America, a single-issue comic based on the Steed and Mrs Peel seasons was published by Gold Key comics in 1968. Due to copyright issues, however (it appears there are some American superheroes or some such thing which apparently also go by the name of the Avengers), they were not able to call the comic *The Avengers*, but instead had to call it *Steed and Mrs Peel*. This single-issue, all-colour comic contained two stories, 'The Roman Invasion' and 'The Mirage Maker'. The two strips featured are colourised reprints of strips originally published in TV Comic in the UK. What is more interesting is that there are actually two versions of this comic. The first version featured photographs from the series on the front, back, and inside the covers, while the second version only featured Steed and Peel on its front. The other pages were replaced with adverts. All other contents remain the same, as does the cover price of 15 cents.

Gold Key with adverts.

Gold Key
with photographs.

Diana, DC Thomson & Co. Ltd

Costing 6*d* an issue, the girls' comic paper *Diana* was to run an *Avengers* strip during 1967. The strip, being printed in colour, ran for twenty-six issues from issue 199 (10 Dec. 1966) to issue 224 (2 June 1967). A total of eight adventures starring Steed and Mrs Peel appeared during this run. Unlike most British *Avengers* comic strips, the ones in *Diana* were in full colour, and of a much higher standard than many of the other strips the *Avengers* featured in. Emma Peel also appeared on the cover of issue 204 (14 Jan. 1967). A free gift was issued with *Diana* in 1966, 'Diana's Top Secret Diary'. This was a small soft cover booklet, which included photos of *The Avengers* along with those of many other spy TV series.

Diana strip.

Diana free gift.

June strip.

June, Fleetway Publications

An interesting *Avengers*-related strip appeared in twelve issues of *June & School Friend* during 1966. This was a story entitled 'The Growing up of Emma Peel'. Running from issue 52 (29 Jan. 1966), to issue 63 (16 April 1966), this black & white strip story is an oddity featuring a fourteen-year-old Emma Knight (Mrs Peel's maiden name) and her father.

Look In, Independent Television Publications

Several issues of this children's comic / TV listings magazine featured pieces on the series. Photos from the series appeared on 27 Feb. 1971. A two-page feature on Diana Rigg appeared on 11 March 1972, followed by a half-page interview on 6 May 1972. While Issue 22 of 1971 featured a full cover photograph as part of a feature on fictional spies. Original price per issue 5p.

Look In cover.

TV Comic strip.

TV Comic, TV Publications Ltd / Polystyle

The Avengers twice appeared as a strip story in *TV Comic*, the first time featuring the Steed and Mrs Peel teaming, which ran from issue 720 (2 Oct. 1965) until issue 771, originally as two pages but from issue 763 as one page. The second time was from approximately issue 880, featuring the Steed and Tara King pairing, which was to run for nearly a further 200 issues. Some of the later Steed / Tara stories were: (from issue 896), 'The Museum Mystery' (from 908) and 'Tigers of the Desert'. After this, new stories don't appear to have been given individual titles. Original price per issue 7*d* later rising to 4p.

Details for the *TV Comic* annuals were given earlier in this book, but the series also appeared in several of the *TV Comic* holiday specials, starting in 1966 with an untitled four-page black & white strip story featuring Steed and Mrs Peel. *The Avengers* then didn't appear in the Holiday specials until 1969 when they reappeared as an untitled text story featuring Steed and Tara King. Steed and Tara would also appear in both the 1970 and 1971 holiday specials; both of these were once again text stories with illustrations. The 1970 story being entitled 'The Journey of No Return'. The French TV listings magazine *Tele Poche* between 1968 and 1971 ran at various time reprints of the strip stories that had appeared in *TV Comic*.

TV Tornado, City Magazines

While not a regular feature of *TV Tornado*, *The Avengers* did feature in a few issues. Most notable is issue 64, which featured a colour cover portrait of John Steed. Other issues to feature in the series included issue 7, which had a TV quiz on the *Avengers*, while the show features in a quiz in issue 20 and issue 24 had a small feature on Diana Rigg.

TV Tornado cover.

TV Guide (American)

American TV listings magazine dated 21 Jan. 1967. This issue has an Avengers cover and feature on Diana Rigg and the Avengers, entitled 'En Garde!'

TV Guide cover.

Man's Journal.

Woman's Own, 1966

A twelve-page supplement magazine appeared in a 1966 edition of *Woman's Own*, entitled *Man's Journal*, and was devoted to John Steed and the Avengers.

Woman's Mirror, 28 May 1966. Fleetway publications Ltd

This woman's magazine features Diana Rigg on the cover and includes a feature of her inside. There was also a feature on John Bates, the man who designed costumes for Mrs Peel during the 1965 season of the *Avengers*.

Woman's Mirror cover.

The magazine cover shown is for *Weekend and Today*, featuring:

WEEKEND and TODAY — Sixpence — No. 3186 March 16-22, 1966

WIN ANOTHER DAIMLER-JAG OR TWO MINI-COOPERS FOR 3d

TURN TO PAGE 23 FOR A CHANCE TO WIN OUR BIG CAR CONTEST

IT'S HELL FOR THE LEATHER GIRL

Diana Rigg finds her *Avengers* reputation is catching up with her

Weekend and Today cover.

Weekend and Today, Associated Newspapers Ltd
(Issue No. 3186) 16 March 1966. Cover Feature: 'It's Hell for the Leather Girl'. Diana Rigg and the *Avengers*. Original Price 6d.

TV Times, Independent Television Publications
Aside from just containing the TV broadcast details for the series, many issues also contained features on the series and as would be expected, several issues have covers depicting the show as well. Here are a few of the notable issues:
30 Dec. 1960: Partial cover and feature on the new seasons shows on ITV.
26 Oct. 1962: Cover photograph.
20 Sept. 1963: Cover and feature.
24 Sept. 1964: Honor Blackman cover.

TV Times cover.

1964 Christmas Special: Patrick Macnee tells the story of the jokers.

30 Sept. 1965: Cover and feature introducing new *Avengers* girl Diana Rigg.

19 Jan. 1967: Cover feature.

28 Sept. 1967: Cover feature.

27 Feb. 1969: Linda Thorson cover.

23 Oct. 1969: Pull out *TV Times* Special on Diana Rigg. An eight-page magazine devoted entirely to Diana Rigg's career to date. This was a pull-out insert inside the regular *TV Times* issue.

This is but a small quantity of the amount of different magazines and comics to have featured the show around the world, having barely scraped the surface of what is out there.

Records

There were two distinctly different themes for *The Avengers*. Also, the theme's arrangement was slightly different each season and many different recordings of both themes, as well as records recorded by the stars of the series themselves, were released.

Versions of the show's original Johnny Dankworth-composed theme:

Singles

Avengers Theme – Johnny Dankworth and his Orchestra, Columbia DB4695, released August 1961. This is the original version of the theme used during the series' first season.

The Avengers – Johnny Dankworth and His Orchestra, Fontana TF422, released November 1963. A more up-tempo re-recording of the theme by Dankworth. This is the version used during the third season. Neither of these releases appears to have been issued in a picture sleeve.

The second, and most familiar, version of the theme tune was composed by Laurie Johnston. This is the most covered version of the theme. Many of these issues have a picture sleeve depicting the show.

The Avengers – Laurie Johnson Orchestra Pye, TN17015, released December 1965. This is definitely the most well-known arrangement, having accompanied the first Emma Peel season of the show in 1965.

This version was reissued in the USA on Hanna Barbera records, HB470, in 1966. It also saw release in Germany on Pye/Hitton HT300116 and in Canada as Pye Records, PYE806.

Above left: Dankworth Columbia single.

Above right: Johnson Pye single.

Cover versions included the double 'A'-sided release by the Joe Loss Orchestra on HMV/Pop 1500 in 1966, having been paired with a cover version of Thunderbirds, also by the Joe Loss Orchestra.

In Germany the Johnston theme was covered by The Marketts on Warner Bros A5814.

An American cover version of the theme was released by Jerry Murad's Harmonicats on the Columbia label in 1969.

Before moving on to the Extended Player records and the LPs, there were a few singles released by some of the series stars. Most notable is 'Kinky Boots', which saw Patrick Macnee and Honor Blackman teamed up.

'Kinky Boots' – Patrick Macnee and Honor Blackman, Decca F11843, issued in 1964. Originally a minor flop on its 1960s release, this recording has subsequently been re-issued twice, once in 1983, on Cherry 62, then again in November 1990, on London Records, KINKY 1, when it achieved a high position in the UK charts. The 'B'-side was another recording by the pair entitled 'Let's Keep it Friendly'. During the same period Honor Blackman also released an LP (details further on), as well as a solo single

Above left: Joe Loss HMV single.

Above right: German single.

Right: 'Kinky Boots' original.

'Kinky Boots' 1980s issue.

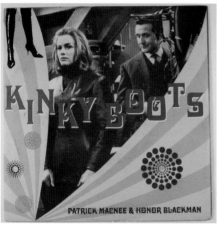

'Kinky Boots' 1990s issue.

'Before Today / I'll Always Be Loving You', on CBS records, CBS 3896, in December 1968.

The next star of the show to produce any recordings was Linda Thorson who, while only producing one single and an EP, seems to have the most different releases of that single. The single was released all over Europe with each country having a different picture sleeve for its issue.

'Here I am / Better than Losing You' – Linda Thorson, Ember EMB S257, issued 1968.

Belgian issue: EMI Columbia DCB 143, release 1968. Some copies of this issue have an over stamp 'Auto Polish 421', which would seem to suggest that this issue of the single was also used in Poland.

French issue: Epic EPC 7063.

Spanish issue: Ember 8500, release 1969.

Dutch issue: Phillips JF 334 578, release 1968.

German issue: Ariola 14214 AT

Unknown issue: Holo DV11873

The final Avengers star to release a single was Diana Rigg, who did so in 1972, when she released 'Forget yesterday / Sentimental Journey' on RCA 2178.

Thorson single, French.

Thorson single, Spanish.

Thorson single, Dutch.

Thorson single, German.

Diana Rigg single.

EPs

Johnny Dankworth's recording of the first season theme appeared on his EP *African Waltz,* issued on Columbia SEG 8137 in 1961, along with three other unrelated tracks.

A cover version of Dankworth's theme appeared on the EP *The TV Thrillers* by Johnny Gregory and his Orchestra in May 1962. This was on Fontana TFE 17389. The other themes covered were *Maigret, Tightrope* and *Johnny Staccato.*

The Laurie Johnston recording appeared on the EP *TV Themes 1966,* PYE NEP 24244, in 1966, with the themes from *The Power Game, The Fugitive* and *The Spies.* A further EP, *TV Themes from Pascall Murray,* MCPS ATV 1, also included the same Laurie Johnston recording. This EP is believed to have been a promotional giveaway. One other EP known

Above left: *TV Themes 1966* EP.

Above right: Pascall Murray EP.

Right: Thorson EP.

to exist is *Temas de TV*, which was released in Mexico in 1969. As well as *The Avengers* theme, this also included themes for *The Champions*, *Department S* and *The Saint*. As well as the single of 'Here I am', Linda Thorson also released an EP. This included 'Here I am' from the single as well as three new tracks, 'You will want me', 'Open up your heart' and 'Wishful Thinking'. This was issued on Ember EMZ006/E in 1968.

Albums

Moving on to LPs and a wealth of recordings appear. *Curtain Up* – Johnny Dankworth and his Orchestra, Columbia 33SX 1572. Dankworth's original recording of the first season theme with several unrelated tracks. This album was re-issued in the USA as a double album, paired with an unrelated Billy Strayhorn album. It saw release on Roulette 9045-121USA, the double album being titled *Echoes of an Era*.

Channel Thrill: The TV Thriller themes – Johnny Gregory and his Orchestra, Fontana TFL 5170/Stfl 585. This album was later on reissued as *The Avengers and Other TV*

Themes – Johnny Gregory and his Orchestra, Wing (Philips) (WL 1087), released in September 1966. This album contains a cover version of the first season theme for *The Avengers*. *The Avengers* – The Laurie Johnston Orchestra. Hanna Barbera. An American album issued in 1966 contained Laurie Johnston's recording along with other unrelated tracks. *Time for TV* – Brian Fahey & his Orchestra. Columbia Studio 2 Stereo TWO 175. Released in 1967, this contains a cover version of Johnston's *Avengers* theme. This LP has a very nice picture sleeve showing *The Avengers*.

Theme from The Avengers – Jerry Murad's Harmonicats, Hallmark CHM 629, released in 1969. Another LP containing *The Avengers* Theme. The same album was issued in America as Theme from *The Avengers* and other TV series – Jerry Murad's Harmonicats on the Columbia label.

Themes and ... – Laurie Johnson Orchestra, MGM CS8104, released March 1969. This has Johnston's arrangement from the final, Tara King season of *The Avengers*. *The Avengers (Theme from the ABC Television Series) and Other Favourites* – Laurie Johnson Orchestra.

Above left: *Channel Thrill!* LP.

Above right: *The Avengers and Other TV Themes*, Gregory LP.

Left: *Time for TV* LP.

Marble Arch Mono MAL695, released 1967. The theme as used during the Emma Peel seasons. Record has very nice picture sleeve showing Steed and Mrs Peel.

Focus on Phase 4 Stereo. BPS 1. 'Phase 4 stereo' released 1968. This is a demo album featuring tracks from several different albums produced by the firm to showcase their stereo recordings. It included the Avengers theme from the album *Themes for Secret Agents*.

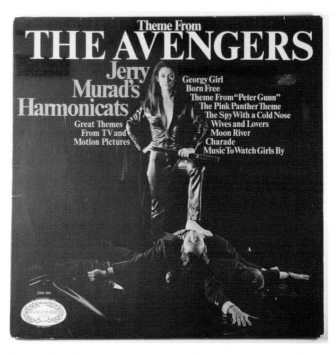

Avengers Jerry Murad LP.

Avengers Laurie Johnston LP, Marble Arch.

Focus on Phase 4 LP.

Themes for Secret Agents, Roland Shaw LP.

Phase 4 World of Thrillers LP.

Themes for Secret Agents – The Roland Shaw Orchestra. 'Phase 4 Stereo' PFS 4094, released 1968. Cover version of Johnston's *Avengers* theme along with versions of several James Bond themes, *I Spy*, *U.N.C.L.E*, *The Saint* and others. *Underworld* – Reg Guest Syndicate. Mercury MCL 20089. Released 1966 features cover version of Johnston theme.

The Phase 4 World of Thrillers – Roland Shaw and his Orchestra. Decca SPA 160. Released in 1971, this features the same cover version of Johnston's theme as used on Shaw's previous album.

The only *Avengers* star that appears to have put out an album is Honor Blackman, who released *Everything I've Got* on the Decca label in the UK in November of 1964, Decca LK/ SKL 4642. It was being released in the USA on the London label in either mono (LL3408) or stereo (PS408).

Blackman LP, UK.

Blackman LP, USA.

Fashion, etc.

Details of fashion released relating to the series are very sketchy. Due to its nature, very little in the way of vintage clothing survives. It is known that several of the outfits designed for Mrs Peel by John Bates also appeared in his ready to wear range under his Jean Varon label. In 1965, an *Avengers* fashion show was held, showcasing many 'Avengerwear' items from the Jean Varon range. This show was featured in a short Pathé newsreel film entitled 'Dressed to Kill'.

Now, from research, it looks possible that there may also have been a fashion show in 1967. Quite possibly this event was run by Edser Southey Design Associates and produced by Michael Edser. This show would have featured the Alun Hughes-designed range of 'Emmapeelers' (Catsuits). Also issued around this time was a range of 'Steed' attire by Pierre Cardin.

Earlier than either of these two fashion shows though, fashion tie-ups with the series had been made. In 1964, Hepworths issued an Avenger Leisure Jacket, designed by Hardy

Fashion labels.

Beret.

50

Amies with promotional materials featuring Patrick Macnee. While readers of *The Viewer* could, in 1963, at a cost of 24s 6d, send off for a dress pattern, ready-to-sew (pre-cut fabric pieces in a choice of five colours), as designed by Frederick Starke for Cathy Gale in the show. This was also the cover feature for that particular magazine. Items believed to have been issued included shoes, hats, gloves, dresses, scarves and bags. In the case of the scarf, it is believed that this was printed silk with an image of Mrs Peel.

Of the items known to have been produced, the target motif beret designed by Bates for Mrs Peel was copied and produced in brown felt (Mrs Peel's original being black and white) by Kangol in 1966. Meanwhile, a mini-dress, originally in black and white, appeared in a red and black version in Varon's own range. John Bates, also as part of his Jean Varon range, designed an Avenger wristwatch; this featured the same black and white target motif on its dial as appeared on the beret. Later on, Old England would issue a range of Richard Loftus-designed watches, several of which would feature both in the series being used by Mrs Peel and in publicity photographs for the series. Old England also marketed certain designs as *Avengers* watches.

Jean Varon watch.

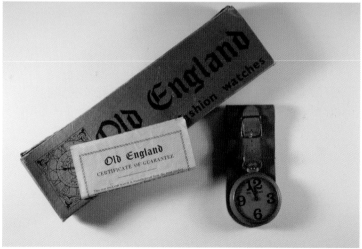

Loftus Old England pocket watch.

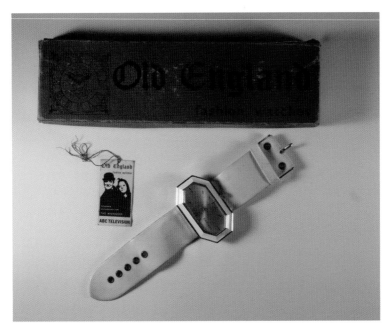

Loftus Old England wristwatch.

Above left: Echo stockings.

Above right: Echo stockings.

 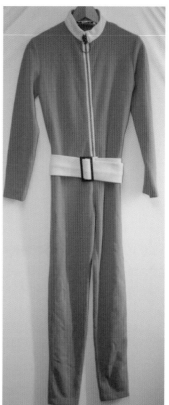

Catsuit.   Catsuit.

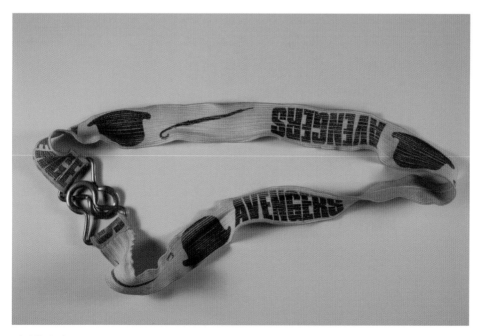

Child's belt.

Echo produced a line of stockings in 1967 with two different packaging designs. A child's belt with brolly and bowler motifs printed on white elastic was produced with a metal clasp. It is believed that these were marketed by Lone Star and were sold loose from a backing card, though no solid evidence to back these claims has yet been discovered.

In the Alun Hughes range, as well as the 'Emmapeelers', a playsuit/dress in green chiffon was produced as well as a green maxi-dress with a paisley type pattern. Even less is known about what appeared from Steed's wardrobe, although it known that Bri-nylon shirts with bowler and brolly motif were produced under the Steed label.

Playsuit.

Maxi-dress.

Promotional and other items

In 1963, Winfield produced a 'pencil pad' exclusively for Woolworths. This small paper pad featured a colour photograph of Steed and Mrs Gale astride a motorcycle.

ABC TV produced at least three different matchbooks. The first appeared in 1961 to promote the Steed and Dr Keel first season, with others promoting the Cathy Gale series and the black & white Emma Peel series. Emma Peel also appeared on a box of matches in Holland.

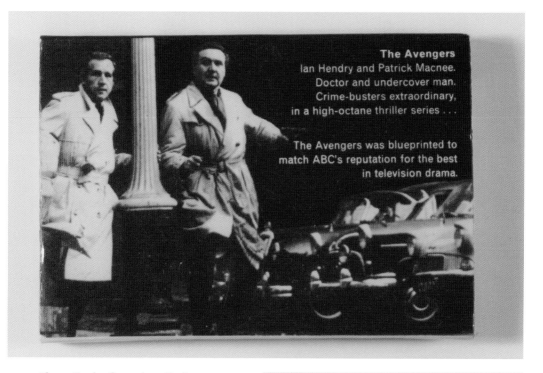

Above: Book of matches, Keel.

Right: Book of matches, Gale.

Above left: Book of matches, Peel.

Above right: Dutch matches.

Above left: Playing cards.

Above right: Invite card / bookmark.

Another promotional item from ABC TV was a pack of playing cards, which promoted the return of Steed and Mrs Peel in colour. Around the same time, individual playing card-like cards featuring Steed and Mrs Peel appeared. These cards feature the same image as was used on the labels attached to some items of *Avengers* fashion and on the Echo stockings packaging, which is why they were previously believed to have been invitation cards to the *Avengers* fashion show. Due to new evidence, it is now believed that these may have been bookmarks that were inserted into editions of the four British paperbacks issued in 1967.

While no trading cards appeared in the UK for the show, two cards did appear in Holland as part of a larger set of TV stars. Also, two small circular cards appeared in Spain. Once again, these probably formed part of a much larger set of various TV stars. Likewise, images of Patrick Macnee and Diana Rigg featured in a set of photos given away with *June* comic in 1965, while Patrick and Linda Thorson featured in a similar set issued by the *TV Times* in 1969.

Two episodes of *The Avengers* featuring Steed and Peel had a cinema release in both France and Germany. Several promotional items can be found from this release, including posters, stills and press-books, while several 8 mm films were produced and sold in Germany featuring Diana Rigg as Mrs Peel.

Dutch cards.

Spanish cards.

TV Times cards.

French poster 1.

French poster 2.

French press book.

Moving into the 1970s and with *The Avengers* no longer on our TV screens, a stage production was mounted in 1971, starring Simon Oats of *Doomwatch* fame as John Steed.

Above left: German press book.

Below left: 8 mm film.

Below Right: Stage show programme.

The New Avengers

Steed returned to our screens in 1976, a little older, but losing none of his debonair style. He was joined by two new, younger companions, Purdey and Gambit. In this new series, filmed as two batches of thirteen episodes (twenty-six in total), Steed largely stayed in the background, leaving most of the action to his protégés. Though this series nowhere near compares to the original series of the sixties, it is still among the finest British TV series of the decade. Well, I say British: it was produced and filmed in England, but it was largely co-financed by the French and Canadians, with four episodes being filmed in both of these countries. The series had a slightly harder edge to it than that of the original, which can be seen particularly in such episodes as 'Dirtier by the Dozen' or 'Cat Amongst the Pigeons', but this was really just a natural development from the original series, bringing it up-to-date for a different era.

The man very much behind this seventies *Avengers* revival was Brian Clemens, who had been involved with the *Avengers* since the beginning. He was to write no fewer than fourteen episodes of *The New Avengers*, co-writing another three, as well as being one of the shows two producers. The other producer was Albert Fennell, another *Avengers* veteran.

Merchandising for this series was just as prolific as it had been during the sixties, though over a more condensed time period. Not only directly related items appeared; Joanna Lumley's likeness was to be used on shop mannequins and cast members were to endorse various products both in the UK and abroad.

Books / Annuals

A series of six books were issued in paperback by Futura Books, with hardback editions being published by Arthur Baker Ltd. Unlike the books issued for the original *Avengers* series, these books were novelisations of various episodes of this new series. The first three issued in 1976 were *House of Cards* by Peter Cave, *The Eagle's Nest* by John Carter and *To Catch a Rat* by Walter Harries. The second batch of three were *Fighting Men* by Justin Cartright, *The Cybernauts* and *Hostage*, both by Peter Cave. In the USA only the first three titles appear to have been published by Berkley Medallion in 1978.

House of Cards also saw publication in Dutch, the only title to do so, as *Het Kaartenhuis*, being translated by Ruud Bal. It was published by *Uitgeverij Ridderhof* in 1976. It was published in Germany in 1978, as *Das Mord-Programme* and in Spain as *Castillo de Naipes* in 1979.

The Eagles Nest was also published in Spain as *El Nido de Aguilas,* while two other titles saw a German publication: *To Catch a Rat* become *Die Weibe Ratte*, and *Fighting Men* become *John Steed und die Grunen Teufel.* Unusual for these European releases is the use

House of Cards, UK issue.

The Eagle's Nest, UK issue.

Above left: *To Catch a Rat,* UK issue.

Above right: *Fighting Men,* UK issue.

Right: *The Cybernauts,* UK issue.

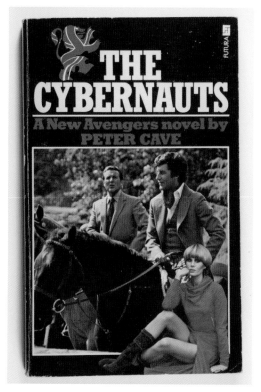

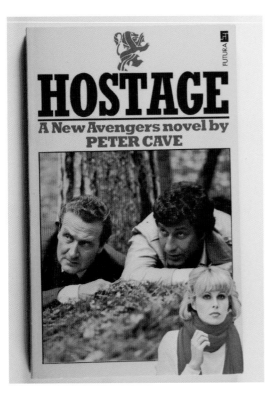

Left: *Hostage*, UK issue.

Below left: *House of Cards*, hardback, UK issue.

Below right: *The Eagles Nest*, hardback, UK issue.

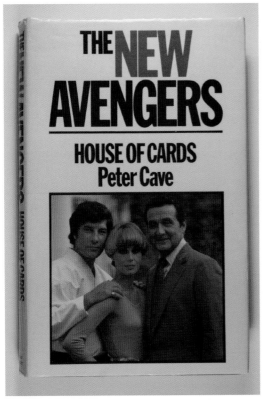

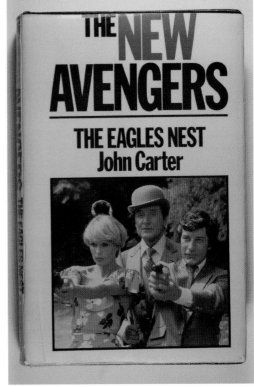

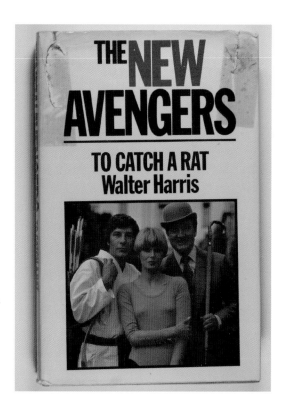

Right: *To Catch a Rat*, hardback, UK issue.

Below left: *Fighting Men*, hardback, UK issue.

Below right: *The Cybernauts*, hardback, UK issue.

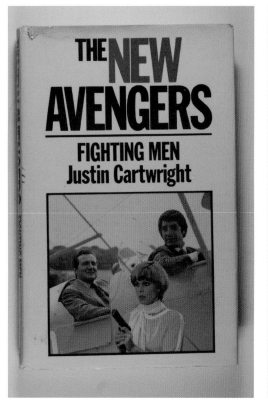

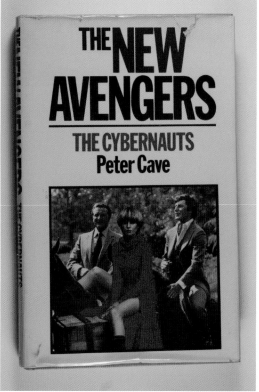

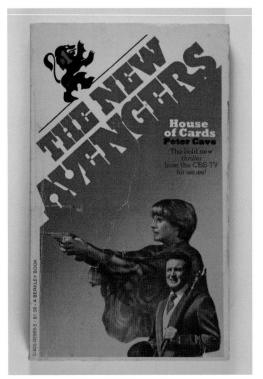

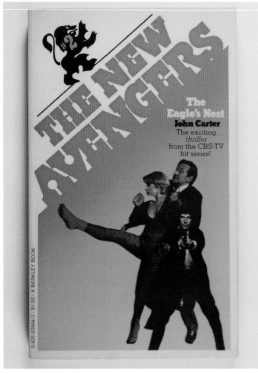

Above left: *House of Cards*, US issue.

Above right: *The Eagle's Nest*, US issue.

Left: *To Catch a Rat*, US issue.

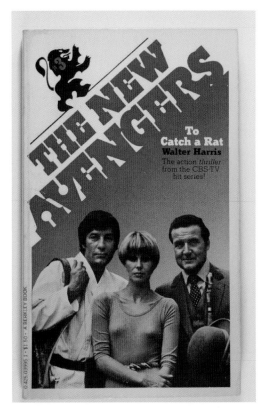

Above left: *House of Cards,* Dutch issue.

Above right: *House of Cards,* German issue.

Right: *House of Cards,* Spanish issue.

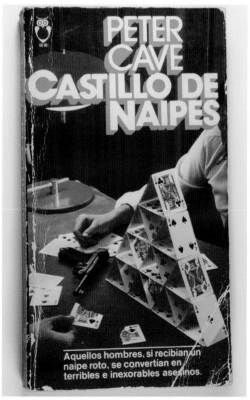

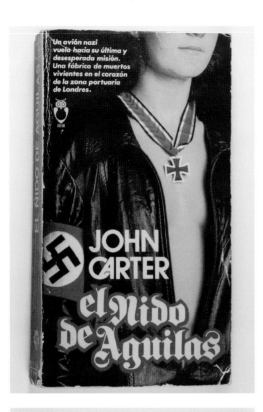

Above left: *The Eagle's Nest*, Spanish issue.

Above right: *To Catch a Rat*, German issue.

Left: *Fighting Men*, German issue.

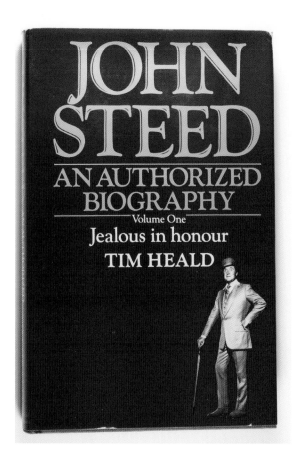

John Steed biography.

of completely unrelated images on the book's cover. One of the German paperbacks even had a still of Steve McQueen on its cover.

Another hardback appeared in 1977, published by Weidenfield & Nicolson. This was *John Steed – An Authorised Biography Vol. 1: Jealous in Honour* by Tim Heald. This tells of Steed's early life up to his first meeting with Cathy Gale. This UK published book is probably one of the rarest *Avengers* books to have been released.

Two annuals were produced by Brown & Watson for 1977 and 1978. Both contained features on the series and the show's three stars as well as text and strip stories. The first has a light blue cover with Steed and Gambit either side of a seated (on the floor) Purdy with the series logo at the top. It contained two strip stories, 'Fangs for the Memory' and 'Hypno Twist', and three text stories, 'A Funny thing happened on the way to the Palace', 'What a lousy way to run a business!' and 'Go and grin somewhere else!'. Original price £1.25.

The second annual has a dark blue cover; all three are standing, with a gun and brolly shown behind and the series logo at the top. It contains two strip stories, 'Midas Secret' and 'The Cybernauts', along with two text stories, 'The Gambit Gambit' and 'A Fluid Situation'. Original price £1.50.

As with the original series, other books / annuals did contain references to the series. The 1979 *Look In Annual* contained a feature on Joanna Lumley, whilst the *TV Detectives Annual* for the same year also contained a feature on the series. Published in 1977 by the

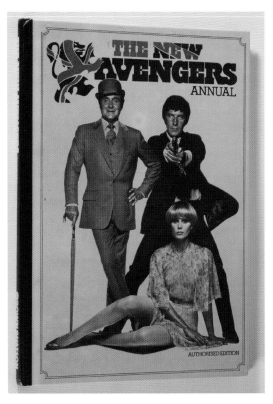

New Avengers Annual 1.

New Avengers Annual 2.

firm Weidenfield & Nicolson, Howard Thomas, who was a top executive and founder of ABC TV, released his autobiography, *With An Independent Air*. This book is notable for its references to the original series as well as its dust jacket, which features the author with Patrick Macnee and Diana Rigg.

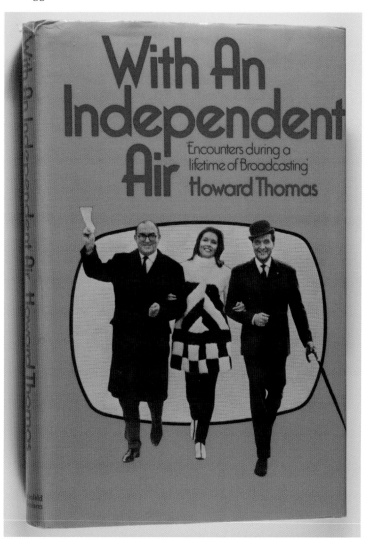

*With An
Independent Air.*

Toys and Games

New Avengers Mission Kit, Thomas Salter, 1976

This kit is so typically mid-seventies in its style with working plastic binoculars, card code wheels, etc. It also has one or two nice touches: the passport (a replica of the now sadly defunct traditional British passport), a 'real working' plastic camera (this could be viewed through a plastic window in the box lid), and a very nice credit card-sized ID card. It also contained a plastic gun, silencer, holster, hand grenade (squirts water), magnifying glass, a plastic camera, paper passport and assorted cardboard cut-outs that made up two code breakers, also a small metal badge.

Mission kit.

Board game, Denys Fisher, 1977

This game is little more than a refined version of Ludo, and as such is very disappointing. Card figures of Steed, Purdy and Gambit are included, as is a rather nice spinner in the shape of a brolly with a bowler hat laid upon it. The game also differs greatly to the prototype shown in the Denys Fisher trade catalogue.

Board game prototype from trade catalogue.

Board game.

Shooting Game, Denys Fisher, 1976

This is a timed target game. Silhouettes of enemy agents are positioned behind windows, in an illustrated street background. The player only has a limited time in which to shoot these targets before a shutter drops in front of the window, blocking his aim. This works on a clockwork mechanism built into the back of the street backdrop. The timer is controlled by a plastic gun-shaped winder attached to the front. This toy also differs from the one shown in the original catalogue, containing both a slightly different target to that shown and a disc-firing gun rather than a suction cup dart gun. A German issue of this set released by Kenner is known to exist, but was not available to photograph for this book.

Shooting game.

New Avengers
Shooting Game

The New Avengers Shooting game captures all the excitement of the top rating ITV series. Any number can play !

Opponents race against the timer and fire safe discs at the targets in the windows before the blinds drop.

But you must remember which are your targets — you'll lose points if you hit the wrong ones ! The winner of the game is the one with the highest score at the end.

12

Shooting game prototype from trade catalogue.

Arrow Games produced a set of four jigsaws in 1976, priced at £1.10 each. All were sized approximately 24 inches x 18 ¼ inches, with each containing 750 pieces. The puzzles are not titled but the illustrated designs were, as such:

1) Steed, Purdey and Gambit in foreground, with a burning building, car & helicopter behind.
2) Purdey kicking a Cybernaut in the face, whilst Steed and Gambit race to the rescue.
3) Cybernaut, Steed, Purdey and Gambit in a montage.
4) Steed leaving 10 Downing Street.

Arrow jigsaw 1.

Arrow jigsaw 2.

Arrow jigsaw 3.

Arrow jigsaw 4.

Purdey Doll, Denys Fisher, 1976

A 10-inch-high plastic doll dressed in purple leotard and black tights, black shoes and a patterned skirt. The figure came bubble-packed on card. This is slightly better than most character dolls as it does vaguely look like who it's meant to be. (But I do stress vaguely!) This to a large degree is achieved by the convincing 'Purdey bob' hairdo. Six further costumes advertised as being available separately included: a rust-coloured jump suit; green halter-neck dress; suede trouser suit with chiffon trimmings, matching hat and scarf; black dress with fur stole; and red cat suit. Appearing in the Denys Fisher catalogues but not issued were action figures of Steed and Gambit.

Purdey doll.

Steed and Gambit

Dressed in his smart suit, bowler hat and carrying that famous umbrella, the John Steed 11½" figure is ready for action-packed adventures! With a pull of the handle, Steed's umbrella converts amazingly to a sword stick and, by operating a button in his back, Steed's fencing arm lunges forward with a cut and thrust action!

The features of the handsome Avenger, Gambit, are captured in this super 11½" action figure! Ready for adventure, Gambit is dressed in his white karate suit which displays his black belt to the full!

By pressing a button in Gambit's back he will deliver a 'stunning' karate chop!

33

Denys Fisher catalogue, Steed / Gambit.

Steed and Purdey did both appear as 12-inch action figures in South Africa, produced by the company Fun World. These were issued in boxes, with the Purdey doll very similar to the Denys Fisher issue in appearance. The Steed figure comes complete with bowler hat and brolly, though truth be told, it looks more like the actor Dennis Price than it does Patrick Macnee. Evidence has been found that Gambit was also issued as a box for this figure, though unfortunately it did not contain Gambit, but another Steed figure.

South African Purdey.
(David Oliver / www.moviebilia.co.uk)

South African Steed.
(David Oliver / www.moviebilia.co.uk)

South African Gambit.
(David Oliver / www.moviebilia.
co.uk)

Two plastic model kits were produced by Revell in 1979: a black and yellow plastic kit of Purdey's TR7 and model kit of Gambit's XJS in red and black plastic. Both kits were produced in 1/25 scale.

Purdey kit.

Gambit kit.

Purdey's TR7, Dinky Toys, 1977

Dinky toy No. 112, die-cast model of Purdey's car. Model is yellow with a black letter 'P' in the middle of the bonnet. Allegedly, a second issue of this model was issued in green with Purdey written in full on the bonnet. It is not known if this version actually exists. There are, however, two versions of the box; the first has a blue and red box header, whilst the second has a wholly red header.

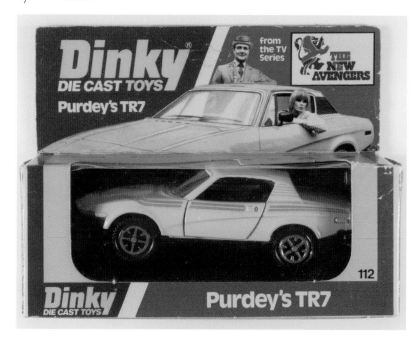

Purdey's TR7.

Purdey's
TR7 box
variant. (Vectis)

Steed's Jaguar. (Vectis)

Steed's Jaguar, Dinky Toys, 1977

This model was to have appeared in blue and it was advertised in the 1978 Dinky catalogue, but it was never officially issued. Over the years, several unboxed examples have appeared, but very few boxed. Those that have appeared were possibly a salesman's samples.

New Avengers Gift Set, Dinky Toys, 1978

This is another product that sadly didn't see official release. It was to have contained both the TR7 and Jaguar, and was advertised in the 1978 Dinky catalogue. Once again, the examples that have surfaced probably only exist as having been traveller's samples.

Dinky catalogue gift set.

Magazines / Comics

TV Times Souvenir Extra, Independent Television Books Ltd, 1976. This was a sixty-eight-page magazine devoted entirely to *The New Avengers* and its origins out of the original *Avengers*.

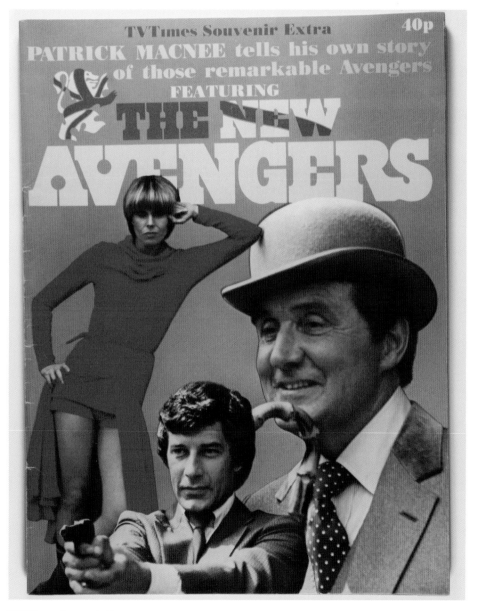

TV Times Souvenir Extra.

Look In, Independent Television Publications Ltd. *The New Avengers* featured on the cover of *Look In* magazine twice. Those issues were: Vol. 6 No. 50 W/e 4 Dec. 1976; Vol. 7 No. 37 W/e 10 Sept. 1977; both issues contained full colour poster pull-outs.

Look In, No. 50.

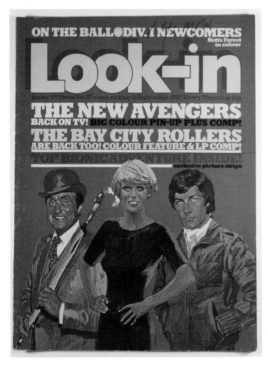

Look In, No. 37.

In France, a single-issue French comic based upon the series was produced in 1977 as *Chapeau Melon et Bottes de Cuir*. In China, eight comics based on the series were produced in 1990.

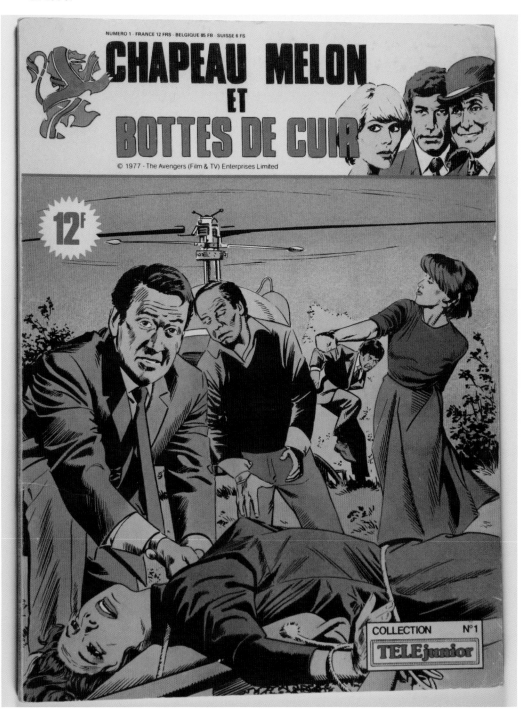

French comic.

Miscellaneous items

Transfers Letraset 1977: A set of rub-down transfers were produced by Letraset with a backing scene based loosely on 'Last of the Cybernauts', which allowed you to create your own picture using the supplied transfers of Steed, Gambit and Purdey.

Scandecor Posters produced a large-sized poster of the trio in 1976. Apparently, both marshmallows and satin sheets were marketed under *The New Avengers* title. Also Kingfisher patches produced a fairly large cloth patch in 1976, which could be either glued or sewn onto its desired location. Joanna Lumley promoted Purdey Perfume in 1976, while Steed appeared on book matches in Germany promoting Polo mints.

All the rage in the seventies were character mirrors, and Origin Gallery Ltd produced two *New Avengers* mirrors in 1976. The first has a black and white photo of Purdey's face printed on the mirror's surface; while the second is a black and white photo of all three cast members, on paper with the mirror overlaid.

Letraset.

Patch.

Mirror, team.

Mirror, Purdey.

Records

Singles

The New Avengers Theme – Laurie Johnson Orchestra, EMI 2562, released 1976. This was also issued in France in 1977 as EMI2c006-98.559. *The Main Themes from both the Professionals and The New Avengers* – Laurie Johnson, and the London Studio Orchestra, Unicorn – Kanchana CI5, released 1980. All three singles were issued in picture sleeves. Of note is that the *New Avengers* theme is the 'B'-side of this record, showing the popularity of its sibling. A flexi-promotional flexi disc of *The Avengers* theme came issued with *Starlog Magazine*.

New Avengers theme, UK issue.

New Avengers theme, French issue.

New Avengers / *Professionals,* single.

Flexi-disc.

Albums

Music from The Avengers, The New Avengers and The Professionals – Laurie Johnson and the London Studio Orchestra, Unicorn – Kanchana KPM 7009, 1980. Side '1' contained music from both original and *New Avengers*, while side '2' contained music from the then brand new series, *The Professionals*. The album came in a photographic gate-fold sleeve.

New Avengers / Professionals LP, UK issue.

Music from The Avengers – Laurie Johnson and the London Studio Orchestra. Starlog / Varese Sarabande ASV9500382. This was the US rerelease of the Kanchana album. Cover versions of the theme appeared on at least these three albums.

20 Great TV Themes – Sounds Orchestral, K-Tel NE 972, released October 1977.

ITV Themes – Stanley Black with London Symphony Orchestra, Hallmark SHM3247, released 1988.

TV Music Spectacular – Burt Rhodes and the London Festival Orchestra. Readers Digest GTVS8B. Released 1978. This was an eight-LP set with *The New Avengers* theme wrongly billed as just *The Avengers*.

Due to space restrictions, this book has been mostly limited to items produced during the original broadcast periods of both shows. But it is worth mentioning that many other items have appeared over the years since the shows ended. Then there was *The Avengers* movie in 1998, which, despite not being well received by many fans, also saw a fair range of merchandise released in its own right. Most notably, there were two fashion ranges. The first was launched by Miss Selfridge in the UK, which saw a vast range of items inspired by outfits worn by Uma Thurman in the movie. The other was by J. Peterman in the US, which saw high-end fashion replicas of the film's costumes. And yet, the merchandise keeps coming; at the time of writing, the firm Unstoppable is due to release a brand new set of trading cards.

New Avengers / Professionals LP, US issue.

ITV Themes LP.